KNIT
TOGETHER

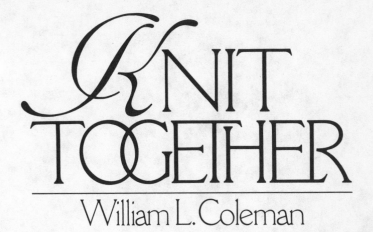

KNIT TOGETHER

William L. Coleman

BETHANY HOUSE PUBLISHERS
MINNEAPOLIS, MINNESOTA 55438
A Division of Bethany Fellowship, Inc.

Photos by Dick Easterday, John Thornberg, Fred Renich, Dan Thornberg, and Chris Torkzadeh.

Published by Bethany House Publishers
A Division of Bethany Fellowship, Inc.
6820 Auto Club Road, Minneapolis, Minnesota 55438

Printed in the United States of America

Library of Congress Cataloging-in-Publication Data

Coleman, William L.
    Knit together.

    1. Marriage—Religious aspects—Christianity—Meditations.
I. Title.
BV835.C6   242′.64   87-6614
ISBN 0-87123-955-8

*To
Pat
on our
24th*

William Coleman

has been married for over twenty years. For ten years as a pastor he counseled many couples during their dating, engagement, and marriage. He has also helped couples whose marriages are in trouble and others who have gone through a divorce.

With his experience as a researcher, writer and speaker, he communicates effectively in the area of family relationships. He has authored nearly three dozen books on a variety of topics.

Contents

EVERY STITCH HELPS

Good marriages are seldom glued, stapled or welded together. The best ones are stitched carefully, deliberately, one stitch at a time. Once marriages have had enough skillful stitches, they are not likely to unravel.

Despite all its bad publicity, marriage is still an unbeatable combination. Though living together without a commitment is prevalent today, couples keep going back to marriage because they know it is one of earth's greatest pleasures and one of God's best gifts—spiritual, emotional, mental as well as physical.

God gave a pattern for cheerful married couples. Hopefully this book will help add a stitch or two to your distinctive and colorful cloth—"knit together in love."

Bill Coleman

Aurora, Nebraska

Perfect Plan

GREAT IDEA

When God created sex,
He came up with
A great idea!

God doesn't get
Nearly enough credit
For this terrific
Program.

Some have mishandled
God's idea.
Others have abused it.
Too many have become
Disillusioned about sex
And have given it up.

Far too many are simply
Misinformed.
Unable to let go and
Learn,
They believe it to be
Evil, weak, silly,
Debasing or empty.

God knew better.
He made sex meaningful,
Rewarding, enjoyable
And fundamentally fun.

God made sex
Guilt-free
In its time,
In its place,
In the marriage
Bed.

God had so many
Good ideas:
Redwood trees,
Waterfalls,
Constellations,
And
People.

Near the top of
The list
Of great ideas
Is married sex.

Good going, God.

"For this reason a man will leave his
father and mother and be united to
his wife, and they will become one
flesh."

       Genesis 2:24

*H*ELD TOGETHER

What holds us together
When we could walk
Away?

What keeps us close
When we are tempted
To drift apart?

Are we held by
Habit,
Finances,
Children,
Relatives,
Hormones,
Or
Fear?

Or are we pulled
Together
By something as basic
As love?

Something as simple,
Something as direct,
Something as mellow,
Something as cheerful
As love.

We can hurt ourselves
By degrading
And belittling
Love
As if it were
Primitive
And defective.

God may have
Created human love
In His finest
Laboratories.

He marks it
With approval.
He recommends it
With pleasure.

If love becomes
Too scientific,
If love becomes
Too analytical,
It loses much
Of its heart.

God furnishes
A healthy
Emotion,
And He calls
It love.

"Love comes from God."
1 John 4:7

BROKENHEARTED

Love is seldom dormant
And hardly ever even.

Love is kinetic
And packed with power.

Because love is
Highly charged,
It is bound to
Backfire
From time to time.

When love backfires,
It hurts—
Enough to break
The strongest heart.

It's all right to hurt
Sometimes.
Love is worth
The risk,
The pain,
The effort.

God understands
Love
That backfires.
He has been hurt
By people
Who gave little
Or no
Response to His love.

God is the authority
On the broken heart.

When it hurts
Too much
To talk,
When the pain
Chokes us
And causes our chest
To ache,
God understands
And stands
Beside us.

Slowly, God
Eases the pain
And holds us
While we cry.

"He heals the brokenhearted and binds up their wounds."
Psalm 147:3

THE BIBLE TELLS ME SO

Whenever we can,
We need to be
Intimate with each other's body.
How do we know?
Just like the children's chorus,
The Bible tells us so.

We need to exult
In each other's flesh,
Meet each other's needs,
Rise up
To each other's expectations.

Not because we are evil,
But because we are smart.
Smart enough to
Keep short accounts
At home.

We need to enjoy
The body of the person
We love.
We need to make
The most of
Breasts and hands
And lips and caresses.
How do we know?
The Bible tells us so.

Our body tells us
We need to touch
Each other.
But we aren't sure whether
To listen or not.
Maybe our body is
Tricking us.
Our body might lead us
Into evil.

How do we know
What it really needs?

Listen to our bodies.
They tell the truth
To married couples.
They want, they need,
They deserve.

Lose yourself
In the body
Of the person
You love,
And feel terrific
About it.

How do we know?
The Bible tells us so.

"A loving doe, a graceful deer—may
her breasts satisfy you always, may
you ever be captivated by her love."
                                        Proverbs 5:19

SECOND–FLOOR CATHEDRAL

Lying on a bed
Late at night
In the dark,
I praise God
For you.

Our bedroom
Became a cathedral
As I offered up
Thanksgiving to God
For all that
You are.

*I thank God for
Tenderness,
Encouragement,
Cheerfulness,
Faithfulness,
Helpfulness,
And all the other
Great qualities
You have.*

*When someone
Means this much,
I have to
Say so.*

*I am too happy
To hold it in.*

*Thank you
For who
You are.*

*Thank God
For making it
All possible.*

*With a full heart
I worshiped God
For sending you.*

"Praise the Lord."

Psalm 150:6

OTALLY FREE

It drives some people
Up the wall.
They can't bring themselves
To believe it.

But the fact is
A married couple
Has absolute, total
Freedom in the bedroom.

Some states pass laws
To control it.
Some people write letters
To deny it.
But the facts remain.
There is total
Moral,
Biblical,
Godly
Freedom in the bedroom.

What a married couple
Agrees to do
And what they enjoy
Is a matter of
Their own taste.

And it is no one else's
Business.
Period.

Freedom frightens
Some people.
Liberty is scary
To others.

How did they become
Dirty words?

What will happen if
A married couple
Is unleashed?

What will happen if
A married couple
Is set free?

What will happen if
A married couple
Is cut loose?

**They might
Get along
Wonderfully.**

*"I am my lover's and my lover is
mine."*

Song of Songs 6:3

*W*HISTLING ALONG

I woke up this morning
With my heart singing.
Humming along, I got
Ready for the day.
By the time I tied
My shoes,
I was whistling.

*Life is good
Because God
Has provided
A great spouse
For me.*

*I don't know how
He did it
And it doesn't really
Matter.*

*All I know is
That God is good,
And my loving spouse
Is proof of it.*

*I'll go off today
With a song in my
Heart.
The song is praise
To God,
And my spouse
Put it there.*

*Sometimes I can't
Figure God out,
But I certainly do
Appreciate Him.*

*"Sing and make music in your heart
to the Lord."*

Ephesians 5:19

Wonderful Words

WHAT SEX SAYS

Sex is more than
A charge,
A thrill,
A high,
A visit
To ecstasy,
Though it can be
All of that
And more.

Over the long run,
Day after day,
Sex is at its best
Because it communicates.

Sex says you are
Worth loving.
Sex says you are
Welcomed
Into someone's intimate
World.
Sex says I want you
Totally, completely,
Without reservation.

Sex talks—
Not merely in grand,
Thundering tones.
Sex speaks
Quietly, confidently.
Sex says things
That words can only
Hint at.

Sex tells us
There is a haven
Where two lovers
Can go
And feel accepted,
Wanted, appreciated,
Needed and satisfied.

Sex may meet
A physical need.
But sex performs
An emotional miracle
By what it says.

Sex says you are
A special garden
And your lover
Will be pleased
To enjoy its fruit.

"Let my lover come into his garden
and taste its choice fruits."
                    Song of Songs 4:16

UNDIVIDED ATTENTION

Turn the radio off.
Put the paper down.
Give the T.V. a rest.

I want to hear you—
And hear you alone.

Send the children
Out to play.
Take the telephone
Off the hook.

I want to listen
To your voice—
And yours alone.

I want to hear
How you feel
And know what
You think.

UNDIVIDED ATTENTION

Tell me
What your heart
Feels,
What your mind
Wonders,
How your soul
Hungers.

Put the car keys
Back.
Close the door.
Be late
For your next
Appointment.

Share with me
What makes you
Laugh.
Remind me
What makes you
Upset.

I want to hear
Your voice
And keep in touch
With
Your spirit.

"Show me your face, let me hear
your voice; for your voice is sweet,
and your face is lovely."
                    Song of Songs 2:14

SPEAK UP!

Has it been too long?
Did we get too busy?
Have we become too involved
To do our homework?
Don't forget to speak up!

Is there something you wanted
That we used to do
But we have let it slide
And let our bed become dull?
Don't forget to speak up!

Were we thoughtless,
Failing to stay around
To hold each other
And snuggle contentedly
In each other's arms?
Don't forget to speak up!

Were we in a hurried rush,
Too preoccupied to slow down
And be careful
And be helpful
And be tender?

Is there something new,
Something meaningful,
Something pleasurable
You would like to try?
Don't forget to speak up!

Trying to guess
What our lover
Needs, wants and feels
Is a tough game
Where couple's hearts
Easily get bruised.

Thanks for taking care
Of our affection
By speaking up!

"A time to be silent and a time to
speak."

Ecclesiastes 3:7

GOOD WORDS

Thanks for using words
Like building blocks.
For being careful to say
Things that are solid,
Supportive and strong.

Good Words

It seems to come naturally
To you.
Healthy words flow
From your mouth
Like a steady, rippling brook.

Good words never appear
Forced or strained
Coming from you.
They sound sincere
And loving.

They must come
From a heart
That wants to share
Its wholesomeness.

God has given you
The gift of good words.
And you are faithful
In spreading your gift
Around.

Thanks for bringing them
My way.

"The tongue of the righteous is
choice silver."

Proverbs 10:20

$\mathcal{F}$EELING GOOD

We make better lovers
When we feel good
About ourselves.

When we feel strong
And confident
And worthy
And lovable.

All day long
We choose our words
Carefully.

We select compliments,
We arrange phrases,
We drop hints
That will make
Our partner feel good.

Filled with the feelings
Of love,
We overflow
And pour our love
On the person
We love.

All day long
We choose words
Aimed at building up.
Geared to lift
The loved one high
Into the clouds.

We avoid picking
And criticizing
And degrading.

Cheerful words make
Cheerful people.

Painful words make
Pained people.

All day long
We release
Each other
With loving words
Designed to create
A beautiful person.

At night
That beautiful person
Will overflow.

"A cheerful heart is good medicine,
but a crushed spirit dries up the
bones."

Proverbs 17:22

MAKING UP

It's one of those
Spiffy sayings that
Every person should
Have monogrammed
On his shorts.
Or maybe tattooed
In an appropriate place.

"Making up
Is a key to
Making out."

It may not be
The only key,
But without it
The door to love
Remains locked.

Friction, anger,
Grudges, spitefulness,
Resentment, jealousy,
Hostility
Slow love down
Or stop it
Altogether.

Making up
Is a key to
Making out.

Each of us knows
It is a fact.
We know it almost
By instinct,
And still we resist
The truth.

Like an icy glacier,
We refuse to melt—
Rigid, cold, immovable.

To melt is
To enjoy.
To melt is
To find
Great pleasure.

Yet we wait,
Hold off,
Punish ourselves
Because
We are too
Stubborn
To do
What is best
For both
Of us.

Making up
Is a key to
Making out.

And the sooner
The better.

"Now instead, you ought to forgive
and comfort him."
2 Corinthians 2:7

COMING TO BED ALONE

Thanks for coming to bed
Alone.
It would have been easy
To bring
The day's problems with you.
Easy to think about
Committees,
Finances,
Repairs,
And appointments.

But you didn't!
You came all alone.

COMING TO BED ALONE

We were there for
Each other.
We didn't have to
Compete
With ghosts of
Pressures.

Bedrooms are made
For two
When you are
In love.

Visitors, guests, creditors,
Relatives, employers
And even children
Have to be left
At the door.

Thanks for clearing out
Your head
And coming to bed
Alone.

"But a married man is concerned
about the affairs of this world—how
he can please his wife."
1 Corinthians 7:33

HOLD ME

Don't say anything.
Don't try to reason
With me.
Don't try to change
My mind
And make me feel better.

Don't tell me how
Things will improve
Or that tomorrow
Will be brighter.

Don't try to sound brave.
Don't try to be clever.
Don't try to be perky.

Just hold me!
Hold me close,
Hold me tight,
Just hold me!

Hold Me

I know the facts;
I don't need information.
I know the answers;
I don't need advice.
What I need now
Is not mental.
I need to know
Someone cares.
Cares enough
To hold me,
And run fingers
Through my hair,
And touch my skin
And be close.

Sometimes we need
To talk it out
Or find a solution
Or take action.

But not now.

Hold me close,
Hold me tight,
But
Just hold me!

"A time to embrace."
Ecclesiastes 3:5

Magnificence Manifested

UP CLOSE

I've watched
A Christian up close.

Not a flashy Christian,
Not the kind
Who is always
Organizing,
Promoting
Or
Committeeizing.

I've seen your patience
With children.
I've watched you sit
By the hour
With the elderly.
I've known you
To feed the hungry.

I've watched
A Christian up close.

You have found
Hope in meditation,
Strength in prayer,
Guidance from the Bible.
Not a bossy Christian
Telling others
What they should do,
Never pushy,
Condemning,
Pontificating.

I've seen your cheerfulness,
Your readiness,
Your eagerness
To help others
Of all kinds,
Persuasions and
Backgrounds.

I've seen a Christian
Up close
Who cannot be labeled
By trendy slogans.

I've seen a spouse
Serve Jesus Christ,
And it moves my heart.

"Each one should use whatever gift
he has received to serve others,
faithfully administering God's grace
in its various forms."
                    1 Peter 4:10

NICKS AND SCRATCHES

She has an oak chair.
It's a child's chair
She has had
Since she was a girl.

Her children play
With it;
The neighborhood children
Climb on it and
Carry it into
The yard.

The chair takes
Some rough treatment.
It collects its share
Of nicks and scratches.

She likes the chair
So much that
She repaints it
Every year.

After that
You can't see
The nicks and scratches.

She doesn't want
A new chair.
She is happy
To paint over
The old one.

The chair
Reminds her of
Her husband.

He messes up,
Says some
Dumb things,
Forgets when
He should remember.

Once in a while
He does something
That is almost
Mean.

She doesn't want
A new husband.
She merely paints
Over the old one.

She covers him
With a fresh coat
Of love.
And he sparkles
Like new.

"Love covers over a multitude of
sins."

1 Peter 4:8

SCHOOL'S OPEN

God wanted to teach me
About peace.

So He sent you
To sleep in my arms
And breathe deeply
On my shoulder.

God wanted to teach me
About joy.

So He sent you
To laugh by my side
And smile broadly
Like a happy child.

God wanted to teach me
About mercy.

So He sent you
To forgive me
When I really
Foul up.

*God wanted to teach me
About sacrifice.*

*So He sent you
To give more than
Your share
And then some.*

*God wanted to teach me
About love.*

*So He sent you
To care about me
And the life
I lead.*

*God wanted to teach me
About commitment.*

*So He sent you—
And you stayed.*

"Follow my example, as I follow the example of Christ."
                                        1 Corinthians 11:1

YOU STAY ALIVE

Thanks for staying alive.
You have not let
Your spirit die.
You have refused to let
Your heart
Turn to stone.

Thanks for keeping the hope
Of a child,
The adventure of youth,
The cheerfulness of optimism.

Your nature bubbles
With the wellspring of life.
You believe in living
And look forward to it
Each day.

You shake off bitterness
Because you know it kills.
You reject disappointment
Because you know it cripples.

Each day is a new beginning.
Every morning is an invitation
To start over.
And you accept it
As a gift from God.

Thanks for staying alive.
Your spirit is contagious,
Your openness infectious,
Your attitude communicable.

God seems to run
A spring to your heart
That ripples with
Hope and goodwill.

You accept it gladly
And drink deeply
From it.
And I am better off
Because you
Bubble over.

"Above all else, guard your heart, for
it is the wellspring of life."
Proverbs 4:23

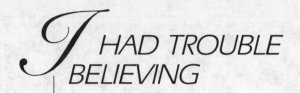 HAD TROUBLE BELIEVING

I had trouble believing
In a God who
Loved me all the time
Exactly as I was.

But then I met you
And learned new dimensions
Of love.

I met you
And saw love working
Every day.

I had trouble believing
In a God who
Gave me grace
That I could not
Earn or buy.

I HAD TROUBLE BELIEVING

Trouble believing in a God
Who gave
Whether I gave back
Or not.

I had trouble,
But it became easier
As I grew to
Know you
And saw how
Giving you are.

I've seen a little
Of the grace of God
In the flesh.
Seeing it in you
Makes it easier
To believe
And accept.

I had trouble believing,
But then I met you
And saw love working
Every day.

"She will set a garland of grace on
your head."

Proverbs 4:9

ARK IT OUT!

Do you remember the day
When I laughed at the cookies
You baked,
Only to discover you weren't
Laughing?

Thanks for marking out
My mistake
And never bringing it up
Again.

Love cannot grow
On broken pottery.
It cannot flourish
On twisted junk.

Do you remember the time
When I yelled at you
And cut you down?

You probably don't remember
Because you are good
At crossing out the past
And moving on
In the sunshine.

You should teach a class
About forgiveness,
Write a book on how
To forget,
Hold a seminar on when
To drop
Yesterday.

Jesus has taught you well
The pleasure of forgiveness,
And you have passed it on
Into our marriage.

"It keeps no record of wrongs."
1 Corinthians 13:5

THOUGHTFULNESS

We've read a dozen books
About marriage.
Even taken a test or two
Just to see
How we were doing.

Went to a seminar,
Listened to a tape,
Made notes so we could
Discuss it later.

We wanted to learn
How to hold together,
How to make it work,
How to be close.

We are a progressive couple,
Aware partners,
Sensitive companions.

Through it all
We found a basic—
An ingredient that
Held everything else
Together.

Lovers who are thoughtful
Have a beautiful relationship.
Partners who are selfish
Tear a marriage to shreds.

Thoughtfulness carries its own
Splendor.
Selfishness is as ugly as
An oyster.

No matter what other
Strengths we have going,
None will cover
The stench
Of selfishness.

Thoughtfulness carries
A beauty that
Begins inside
And pushes
To the surface.

"Each of us should please his
neighbor for his good, to build him
up. For even Christ did not please
himself."

Romans 15:2, 3

Positive Possibilities

WILLING TO LEARN

When you get married,
You know a lot about sex,
And most of it is wrong.

We learn from television,
Movies, jobs, rumors and magazines,
And most of it is wrong.

We hear about stereotypes—
That women are like this
And men are like that,
And most of it is strange.

Smart couples want to learn
What sex is really like
And not what myths
Claim it to be.

They teach each other
In the bedroom.
They hold classes for
Each other
With open minds
And willing spirits.

*They are not afraid
To learn the truth
About each other
And themselves.*

*They accept total intimacy
As natural, healthy,
Rewarding and loving.
They give and take
In the school of love.*

*Smart couples read
Material that is accurate,
Material that is positive,
Material that is helpful.*

*Unwilling to fumble along
With misinformation,
They are determined to
Find out
And enjoy sex completely.*

*Knowledge is the friend
Of marriage.
The more we know
The better we love.*

"The discerning heart seeks
knowledge."
Proverbs 15:14

WHO'S DRIVING?

I've shoveled coal
And I know
It isn't a passion.
I was never drawn
To it.
Shovels are easy
To put down
And leave.

I've unloaded wood
And I know I could
Get along fine
Without it.
If I never emptied
Another boxcar,
I'd die a happy man.

There was no driving force,
No instinctive call
To break one's back all day.

But sex—
That's a different story.

God placed in most
A driving force
To make contact,
To make love,
To make out,
To make children,
To make happy.

He took no chances
That we might acquire
A taste for it.
He built it into
The original material.

Sex is factory-installed.
It isn't an option
Offered to the owner.
We can't swap it
For whitewalls.

That's why it's called
A drive.
It's a force,
A magnet
That draws us
Together.

Like all drives,
It needs a driver.
God expects us
To take hold
Of the controls.

But He does expect us
To drive it
And He wishes us
Happy motoring.

"For love is as strong as death, its jealousy unyielding as the grave. It burns like blazing fire, like a mighty flame."

Song of Songs 8:6

$\mathcal{B}$E PATIENT

I'm not always
Considerate
When you don't
Feel well.

Often I don't even
Stop
To think how you
Might feel.

ℬE PATIENT

I'm not always
Quiet
When you have
Something
You want to say.

I like the sound
Of my own voice
And the patter
Of my own stories.

But don't give up
On me.
Change comes slowly.
But I do want
To change
For you.

I need to learn
To anticipate
What you face,
So I can help
Rather than stand
Around,
Like a moose.

I want my mind
To create
Ways
To make your
Life
Go well.

And I want it
To go well
Because
I love you.

I want to
Get better
At loving
You.

Be patient!
I'm getting there.

"Love is patient."
        1 Corinthians 13:4

GOOD FIGS

Gardens left alone
Become victims
Of the weeds.

They are choked
And dwarfed
From neglect.

Fruit trees
Left to themselves
Are soon overrun
By insects and disease.

Carefully pruned,
Sprayed
And harvested,
They produce
Ripe, firm fruit,
Enough to please
The owner.

Marriages left alone
Become overgrown,
Unmanageable and
Shabby.

Before long it is
Unsightly and
Uncomfortable
For everyone.

Love calls out
To be tended,
Cultivated,
Weeded,
And nurtured.

Love blossoms,
Spreads,
And reproduces
When it is
Faithfully
Attended.

"He who tends a fig tree will eat its fruit."

Proverbs 27:18

JUDGING SLOWLY

We live too closely,
We share too intimately,
We talk too honestly
To ever begin to judge
Each other.

We know each other
Too well,
And we reach each day
To know
Each other even better.

If we are quick
To judge,
We will retreat
Into our shells.

We venture out
More each day
Because we trust
And are not afraid
Of being judged
Too quickly.

"Do not judge."
Matthew 7:1

HYPERBOLE ME

I love it when
You say wonderful things
About me
That aren't quite true.

When you talk
About my looks
And my talent
And, oh yes,
My bedroom eyes.

We both know
You stretch it,
But I love it
When you
Hyperbole me.

Read about the lady
In the Song of Solomon.
She said her lover
Had eyes like doves
And cheeks
Like beds of spice.

She knew how
To turn him
Into putty.

Go ahead,
Tell me.
Talk about
My hair,
My forehead,
And don't forget
My eyebrows.

I know you
Wouldn't lie
To me,
But I love it
When you
Hyperbole me.

Tell me
How strong
I am.
Ask me
To open the jars
For you
And carry out
The heavy trash.

I love it
When you
Hyperbole me.

(Pour it on, lady.)

"His arms are rods of gold set with
chrysolite. His body is like polished
ivory decorated with sapphires."

Song of Songs 5:14

⨡OAP AND SEX

Roses and candlelight
Are hard to beat
To set a romantic tone.

Gentle whispers and
A bit of nibbling
On the ear
Can be just
The right ticket.

But day in
And day out
You can't do better
Than a good bar
Of soap.

There is no aphrodisiac
Like the clean, fresh
Body
Of the person you love.

No turn-on like
The smell of newly
Shampooed hair.

There are exceptions.
Some days you could
Make love
To your partner
Even if he has
Just finished
Working overtime
In a coal mine.

But that's the rare
Exception.

When lovers
Come to bed,
They should be ready
For anything.

A good bar of soap
Helps make sex
Go a lot better.

"He is altogether lovely."
                    Song of Songs 5:16

HAPPINESS IS A CHOICE

Happy people
And unhappy people
Have the same amount
Of setbacks.

Their drains clog
Just as often.
The dog digs
In the flower gardens
Of the righteous
And the unrighteous.

Paint peels
For Baptists
And Lutherans
At the same
Rate.

The big difference
Between people
Is that some
Choose to be
Happy
While others
Decide to be
Unhappy.

Life becomes
A question
Of attitudes,
Of hope,
Of faith.

Setbacks cannot
Destroy love.
God made us
Far too strong
For that.

Troubled waters
Cannot drown out
Compassion
Between two people
Who care.

God made us
Far too tough
For that.

Happy couples
Tie everything down,
Reach for each other,
And ride out
The storms.

God made us
Like that.

"Many waters cannot quench love."
Song of Songs 8:7

DOWN TO A SPARK

It was almost out.
Not much left
But a few embers.
Barely enough to spit out
A spark once in a while.

Seldom does it burn
That low.
But left untended,
Forgotten, even ignored,
The flame goes out
Leaving little warmth.

Smothered in ashes,
Half buried under
The charred wood,
Love all but fades
If we aren't careful
To give it fuel.

But each time
God gave us
Enough sense
To bring dry paper,
Crisp twigs
And seasoned wood
To call it back
To life again.

The fire in our love
Has burned low
From simple neglect.
We have nearly choked
It off
From lack of air.

But the spark
Always stayed
And rose into
Dancing flames
Again.

Thanks for
Never losing sight
Of the spark.

"Consider what a great forest is set
on fire by a small spark."
James 3:5

CASTING BREAD

We could have
Played it safe,
Taken no chances,
Done the predictable,
The quiet, the dull.

But if we had lived
No adventure,
We would never
Have known
An exciting career,
The mountains of Colorado,
The tents of Canada,
The jungles of Belize,
The Fort George Hotel.

If we had lived
No adventure,
We would have had
No children,
No ministries together.

*We would have
Learned so little
About God
And the way
He works.*

*We haven't cast
Our bread
On the waters
Often enough.
But when
We have cast it,
We have been glad
We lived the adventure.*

*Adventures in faith,
Adventures in creativity,
Adventures in love
For each other.*

*Marriage is one
Of life's great adventures.
And we are glad
We launched out.*

We would have
Missed too much
Just playing it safe.

"Cast your bread upon the waters,
for after many days you will find it
again."

Ecclesiastes 11:1

Painful Pitfalls

No More Candles

It sounded like
A solid plan.
Why not turn off
The lights
And make love
By candlelight?

She thought it was
So romantic—
Subdued lights,
Soft whispers,
Tender motions,
Gentle caresses.

What couple could
Resist it?
The launching pad
To an evening of
Bliss.

Soon after everything
Was in place—
Warm, snuggly, intimate—
She thought again
And decided the candle
Needed to be moved.

Carefully she reached
Across his body
And picked up
The glowing candle.

Moving the candle
Over his body,
She slipped.

Hot wax cascaded
Down
Onto his waiting
Body.

A blood-curdling scream
Rang out
Through the night.

And the neighbors
Merely shrugged
Their shoulders.

"Break forth and cry aloud."
Galatians 4:27

LEFT HANGING

Speak to me.
Tell me what
You want.

If you get upset
And refuse to say
Why,
I feel like Absalom—
Left hanging
In midair.

Don't ask me
To guess
What you need.
Don't expect me
To read your mind.
I can't anticipate
What you might
Be thinking.

Speak to me.
Tell me what
You want.

I can't be Absalom
Hanging in midair.

"Absalom's head got caught in the
tree. He was left hanging in midair,
while the mule he was riding kept
on going."
                           2 Samuel 18:9

$\mathscr{P}$ICKING FIGHTS

Some couples like
To pick berries,
Apples and tomatoes.

Others spend most
Of their time
Picking fights.

As if they saw
Quarreling
As a sign that
They were alive.

Could life be
So dull
And empty?
Could life be
So tasteless
That we have
To fight
To give it
Purpose?

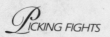

*Some couples like
To pick flowers,
Vacation routes
And candidates.*

*Others spend most
Of their time
Picking fights.*

*Do some have
To hear their voices
Yelling
To know
They are alive?*

*Are some so
Desperate
For attention
That they must
Quarrel
To gain affection?*

*Some couples like
To pick colors,
Names and houses.*

*Others spend most
Of their time
Picking fights.*

*"It is to a man's honor to avoid
strife, but every fool is quick to
quarrel."*
                    Proverbs 20:3

NAGGING DELILAH

Good partners
Make it a point
To communicate.

When something
Goes wrong,
They talk about it.

When something
Needs to be
Corrected,
They are careful
To mention it.

Smart partners
Never nag at
Each other,
Or pick,
Or prod,
Or drive
Each other
Nuts.

It's unhealthy
To constantly
Pull
At the person
We love.

If we do it
Too long,
We begin
To pull
Him apart.

Samson didn't die
From having his
Hair cut.

The muscle man
Wasn't even
Tortured to death.

A collapsing temple
Would not have
Been enough
To do him in.

Samson really died
Because Delilah
Nagged him to
Death.

"With such nagging she prodded
him day after day until he was tired
to death."

Judges 16:16

ONEY TALK

Married couples always have
Something to talk about.
At least one subject
Never goes away.

Day in and day out
Couples talk about money.

Even couples who love
Passionately
Find themselves
Sometimes strained
And drained
Over money.

For most of us,
There is never enough
And never will be.

Some couples
Set goals.
But as soon
As they get
Near them,
They move the goals
Farther away.

Frustrated,
They can never
Make enough,
Spend enough,
Save enough,
Pay enough
Soon enough.

Built-in tension
In a world that
Will never have
Enough money.

Beautiful relationships,
Parched by the thirst
For more money.

"Whoever loves money never has
money enough; whoever loves
wealth is never satisfied with his
income. This too is meaningless."
Ecclesiastes 5:10

GUARD OUR LIPS

Running people down
Makes us feel dirty.
It seems to take
The shine off
Our time together.

It's like having
A film on your teeth
After eating something
Greasy.

We do it,
Like others,
But it leaves
A bad taste.

God, help us
Do it
Less and less.

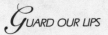

Hearts filled
With love
Have no room
For ugliness.

Guard our lips
By filling
Our hearts
With love.

"The words of a gossip are like choice morsels; they go down to a man's inmost parts."
Proverbs 26:22

# BOXCARS

Don't be content
To be
A boxcar
On my train.

Don't make me
The engine,
Pulling you along
Up hills
And around curves.

You are your
Own engine.
You must travel
Your own tracks
And cover
Your own territory.

Your gifts
Are not
My gifts.

Your ministry
Is not always
My ministry.

Boxcars

Don't surrender
Your visions
To become
A boxcar
On my train.

You are an engine,
Not a boxcar.
You have your own
Power, purpose
And plan.

Most of the time
Our engines travel
Together.
But not always.

Use your gifts.
Help your people.
Defend your causes.
Speak up with
Your voice.

You have too much
To offer.
Never stop being
An engine
To become
A boxcar.

"We have different gifts, according
to the grace given us."
                                    Romans 12:6

*W*HAT THE DOCTOR ORDERED

We spend too much time
Sitting,
Too much time reading,
Eating,
Watching television.

When you sit too much,
The heart
Slows down
And forgets
How to pump hard.

We begin to stagnate,
Fossilize,
Petrify,
And crust over.

We need more activities
That cause our hearts
To speed up, race
And romp along.

That's one more reason
Why
We are good for each
Other.

We cause each other's
Hearts
To pound.

Sometimes to pound
Slightly,
Sometimes to pound
Moderately,
Sometimes to pound
Like thunder.

Heart pounding is
An honorable
Pastime.
It's done by nearly
All good couples.

W*HAT THE DOCTOR ORDERED*

*If heart pounding
Is done too seldom,
It could be dangerous
To your health.*

*To offer the maximum
Benefit,
Hearts must pound
Frequently.*

*Pounding hearts
Tend to make
Long-lasting couples.*

"My heart began to pound for him."
    Song of Songs 5:4

*F*ORGET THE STATS

It's possible to be
Overly educated about sex,
To know too much
For our own good.

Some people know
What percentage of
Husbands have affairs,
And it scares them
Till it hurts.

Others have heard
How often
The average couple
Has sex.
And so they aim
To have it
At the rate
Of 2.3 times
Per week.

They soon discover
It is
The .3 times
That is really difficult.

It must be miserable
To map out our love life
By the statistics.

We all want to be normal.
We each want to be average.
But we lose the fun
Of being ourselves.

Some study sex
Too little.
Others study sex
Too much
And take it
Far too seriously.

At our best
We are lovers,
Not trendies.

At our best
We are romantics,
Not categories.

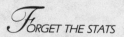

At our best
We are passionate,
Not perfectionists.

At our best
We are ourselves.

Let us be ourselves
And enjoy each other.

"Eat, O friends, and drink; drink your fill, O lovers."

Song of Songs 5:1

Terrific Teammates

TIME OUT

No agenda, no schedule
To keep.
Just getting away
For the day.

No problems, no goals
To set,
Just driving away
For the day.

Two of us alone
In a car,
Riding through
The sandhills.

No radio to keep
Us company,
No tapes to serenade.

Talking, laughing,
Looking at
The canyons,
Watching an eagle
Circle above
A valley.

Taking time out
To enjoy each other,
Like teenagers dating,
Drinking each other in
As part of the scenery.

A few bucks
For gas,
A few bucks
For a meal
Of sausage and eggs.

It wasn't
A Caribbean cruise
Or a flight
To Tibet.
It was just
Time out.

**Time out
To be together
And drink in
Each other's
Company.**

*"Come with me by yourselves to a
quiet place and get some rest."*
                    Mark 6:31

A LOT IN COMMON

They have a lot
In common.
They both enjoy
Crab legs,
Good books
And Bill Cosby.

They like to
Travel,
Walk across
The plains
And eat
Reuben sandwiches.

They miss
Their children
From time
To time
And love
A crackling fire.

They don't appreciate
War,
Injustice,
Abuse,
Hunger,
Or
Plumbing
That won't
Shut off.

They both believe
In Jesus Christ
And try to follow
Him.

They follow
And believe
Haltingly,
Unsteadily,
Brashly,
And sometimes
Boldly.

They have
A great deal
In common.
Their commonality
Makes love
All the stronger.

"If you have any encouragement
from being united with Christ, if any
comfort from his love."
Philippians 2:1

_L_ATE FOR WORK

She was late
For work.
That's a terrible
Feeling,
But it happens
Every now
And then.

Her hair
Wasn't brushed
As neatly
As she would
Have liked.

She would
Have to live
With that
All day.

She felt guilty,
A bit conspicuous,
But she'd get
Over that, too.

Soon she
Began to grin
And think
To herself
About the
Natural blush
In her cheeks
And the extra sparkle
In her eyes.

It was worth it.

Some mornings
It's hard
To get out
Of bed.

Because you love
Each other
Too much.

"How much more pleasing is your
love than wine."

Song of Songs 4:10

GOLFING TOGETHER

Thanks for learning
To golf with me.

You look so happy
Out-of-doors,
Standing in the breeze,
Sun shining
Against your face.

You look healthy,
Bag flung
Over your shoulder
Marching up the hill
To hole three.

You look childlike,
Sprawled
On your stomach
In the mud,
Recovering a ball
From the stream.

You look thrilled,
Sinking a par
On the back slope
Of green four.

You look happy
Out-of-doors,
Out of context,
Out of pressure.

Thanks for learning
To golf with me.
For finding
New fields for us
To share.

Thanks for giving
Life
To our love.

"Listen! My Lover! Look! Here he
comes, leaping across the
mountains, bounding over the hills."
                    Song of Songs 2:8

COME WALK WITH ME

Come walk with me.
Walk by the sea
And share our dreams
For life together.

Come walk with me
In the dancing rain
And smell the cleanness
Filling our lungs.

Come walk with me
On the green hills
And talk to me
Of love and hope.

Come walk with me
Among the trees
And tell me about
The children we
Might hold.

Come walk with me
Across the pavement
And stretch our vision
Over the years
And see ourselves
Mature together.

Come walk with me,
And Jesus Christ
Will walk with us,
And we will be part
Of Him
As He is part
Of us.

*"But if we walk in the light, as he is
in the light, we have fellowship
with one another, and the blood of
Jesus, his Son, purifies us from all
sin."*

1 John 1:7

RUNNING BUTTONHOOKS

It may not have been
Your favorite
Thing to do,
But you were always there.

When we needed an extra
Player for football
In the park,
We could count on you.

You would run pass patterns,
Block your wiry son
Or toss a pass
With all your might.

Anytime we needed someone
To run a buttonhook,
We knew you'd come through—
If we'd explain what
A buttonhook was.

You ran with us
Down the field.
You shouted with us
When we scored.

And you laughed with us
When you slipped in the mud,
Soaked head to foot in
The slime and wet grass.

Then you fixed hot chocolate
While we told war stories
Of how we had just
Made fantastic catches,
Run reverses
And blocked passes.

God has made each wife
Special.
But wives are extra special if
They run buttonhooks.

"He who finds a wife finds what is
good."

Proverbs 18:22

MOTEL MEMORIES

Motels were created for
Happy couples.
Couples who need to
Get away for an evening
And take care of each other.

Couples who have children
Who throw food
And stuff toys down
The toilet.

Couples who have neighbors
With loud stereos
And souped-up Novas.

Motels were created for
Happy couples.
Couples who can get
A babysitter for the evening.
Couples who steal away
For a date
With each other.

Couples who set a place
And a time.
And know exactly
Why they are there—
And love it.

Motels were not made
For foolish couples,
Frightened and looking
For thrills.
Motels were created for
Married couples
Who need some space
For themselves.

Motels were made for
Married couples
Who have enough sense
To invest time,
Money and energy
In each other.

Happy couples
Have mental slides
Of some great
Motel memories.

"Take me away with you—let us
hurry!"

Song of Songs 1:4

BETTER THAN A BLENDER

They could have given us
A set of towels.
You can't get too many
Of those.

They might have presented us
With a blender.
Ours makes a funny noise
And spits through the lid.

But the church board wanted
To be kind
And thoughtful,
So they reached back
Into their imagination
And voted for
Love.

They presented us with
The honeymoon suite
In Lincoln.

Roses,
Music,
Dinner—
Those romantic
Foods.

They voted
For memories,
Tenderness
And love.

It was
So much better
Than a blender.

"That your love may abound more
and more."

Philippians 1:9

AITHFULNESS

Faithfulness: strong as steel.
We can count
On each other
And never have
To wonder.

Faithfulness: steady as stone.
We know
Storms will not
Tear us apart.

Faithfulness: bouncing back.
We get down
But always know
Our love will
Surface again.

Faithfulness: standing together.
We know we are
Never alone
No matter what
The disappointment.

Faithfulness: knit as one.
We choose to believe
The best about
Each other
Because
We choose
Love.

*"Let love and faithfulness never
leave you; bind them around your
neck, write them on the tablet of
your heart."*

Proverbs 3:3

PLANNING THE GOOD TIMES

We have to put it
On the calendar.
Mark it down early
And refuse to let
Anything push it off.

Too much happiness
Gets away
Because we forget
To plan it.

*If we expect
Good times
To just happen,
They have a way
Of getting away.*

*They are squeezed out
By committees,
Television, football,
And save-the-lizard
Campaigns.*

*Good times do come
Spontaneously,
Unexpectedly,
But not quite
Often enough.*

*And good times
Are too important
To leave
To chance.*

*We have to put it
On the calendar.
Mark it down early
And refuse to let
Anything push it off.*

"But those who plan what is good
find love and faithfulness."

Proverbs 14:22

*W*HEW!

Whew!

**Tell the truth.
Doesn't it feel great
To be exhausted
When you're finished?**

"Drink your fill, O lovers."
Song of Songs 5:1